3:16
THE STORY OF GOD

DR. MICHAEL T. GEORGE

A POST HILL PRESS BOOK
ISBN (hardcover): 978-1-68261-060-2
ISBN (eBook): 978-1-68261-061-9

3:16
The Story of God
© 2016 by Dr. Michael T. George
All Rights Reserved

Cover Design by Quincy Alivio

Post Hill
PRESS

Post Hill Press
275 Madison Avenue, 14th Floor
New York, NY 10016
posthillpress.com

Dedication

To God be the glory, great things He has done; so loved He the world that He gave us His Son, who yielded His life an atonement for sin, and opened the life gate that all may go in.

Great things He has taught us, great things He has done, and great our rejoicing through Jesus the Son; but purer and higher and greater will be our wonder, our transport, when Jesus we see.

Introduction

It is a normal Saturday in September when a young man prepares for his autumn weekend ritual. He carefully selects the clothes he will wear. They have been specially chosen for this event. Shoes, socks, hat, and belt; all must coordinate. He wants to make sure there is no doubt about the message being conveyed. He is a football fan and the colors declare allegiance to his favorite team.

With everything prepared and ready to go the young man gets into his vehicle. He carefully places his team flag on the side window before closing the door. It will wave his pride to the world.

While backing out of the driveway he notices a bumper sticker on his neighbor's car. He gives it a glance and then pulls away. It was not a clever message like most, just a combination of letters and numbers. He thinks little of it as he pulls onto the highway.

Racing along with his music at full blast he sees an electronic billboard with a message emblazoned across it. Before he can read the entire slogan the digital display changes. He could not make out the words, but he does remember the numbers he saw: 316.

Finally the stadium is within view. He quickly finds his designated area to park and heads inside to find his seat. It is a beautiful day for football. The sun is shining, the temperature is perfect, and his team is on a winning streak. He has looked forward to this day all week long.

The pre-game ceremonies are in full stride when an airplane flies over with a banner attached to the tail. The message is large and easy to read. Interestingly it contains the same numbers he saw on the bumper sticker of his neighbor's car and the billboard.

As his eyes return to focus on the field he notices someone holding up a sign behind the goal post. He can't quite make it out so he grabs his binoculars to focus in more closely. The sign is folded in half so he cannot see what it says on the top but the bottom clearly displays "316." He slowly begins to ponder these things when he realizes the captains are headed out to mid-field for the opening coin toss.

The large jumbotron on the scoreboard displays the events taking place at the fifty yard line. The camera work is superb, you can see everything in perfect detail. The referee turns to the opposing team asking them to choose heads or tails. As the face of the quarterback comes into view he sees it once again. Painted under the eyes of the opposing team's signal caller are the numbers he has seen all day: 316.

*

If you are a Christian, you recognize these numbers as part of the verse for John 3:16. However, does that chapter and verse combination play a bigger role in the New Testament? Could it be God so ordained His written word so the entire story of His redemption of mankind could clearly be seen in the simple combination of 3:16?

Coincidence or Divine inspiration, that is for you to decide! Welcome to 3:16: The Story of God.

Matthew 3:16

KING JAMES VERSION (KJV)
And Jesus, when he was baptized, went up straightway out of the water: and, lo, the heavens were opened unto him, and he saw the Spirit of God descending like a dove, and lighting upon him:

NEW INTERNATIONAL VERSION (NIV)
As soon as Jesus was baptized, he went up out of the water. At that moment heaven was opened, and he saw the Spirit of God descending like a dove and alighting on him.

ENGLISH STANDARD VERSION (ESV)
And when Jesus was baptized, immediately he went up from the water, and behold, the heavens were opened to him, and he saw the Spirit of God descending like a dove and coming to rest on him;

GOD'S WORD TRANSLATION (GW)
After Jesus was baptized, he immediately came up from the water. Suddenly, the heavens were opened, and he saw the Spirit of God coming down as a dove to him.

The story begins with the heavens openly declaring to the world that God approves of His Son. The saving of mankind and the work of redemption in earnest has now begun!

*

God, the Creator of the universe, looks down upon the earth to observe the baptism of His son, Jesus the Christ. For thirty years Jesus has quietly lived his life, but the appointed time has now arrived for Him to begin his earthly ministry.

The stillness of the water begins to ripple with anticipation as the Prince of Peace enters. If the rocks, trees and sand could cry out in glorious celebration they most certainly would. This sin-cursed world has long been waiting for this event.

John takes the Son of God and slowly lowers Him back into the water until He is fully submerged. The world now stands still waiting for Jesus to reappear from the watery deep.

A jubilant chorus of angels begins to sing in the heavens as Jesus comes up out of the water. As a proud Father, the Holy Spirit of God descends from the heavens in the form of a dove. The Prince of Peace has formally launched His mission to bring hope to a helpless world.

Mark 3:16

KING JAMES VERSION (KJV)
And Simon he surnamed Peter;

NEW INTERNATIONAL VERSION (NIV)
These are the twelve he appointed: Simon (to whom he gave the name Peter),

ENGLISH STANDARD VERSION (ESV)
He appointed the twelve: Simon (to whom he gave the name Peter);

GOD'S WORD TRANSLATION (GW)
He appointed these twelve: Simon (whom Jesus named Peter),

Christ starts His work by assembling a group of a chosen few. He changes the name of Simon to Peter after He transforms him into somebody new.

*

As Jesus begins His earthly ministry folks everywhere are amazed at the healing power of the carpenter from Nazareth. Large crowds follow closely taking every opportunity available just to be near this man of miracles.

Christ could have chosen the religious rulers or noble kings of the time period to be His followers, but this was not to be the case. Instead, he selects the downtrodden, the sinners, and those the world deems common.

His chosen few include tax collectors, tradesmen and ordinary sinners. Simon Peter is just a simple fisherman, before the King of Kings calls to him. His decision to follow the Nazarene will forever change his life.

Luke 3:16

KING JAMES VERSION (KJV)

John answered, saying unto them all, I indeed baptize you with water; but one mightier than I cometh, the latchet of whose shoes I am not worthy to unloose: he shall baptize you with the Holy Ghost and with fire:

NEW INTERNATIONAL VERSION (NIV)

John answered them all, "I baptize you with [a] water. But one who is more powerful than I will come, the straps of whose sandals I am not worthy to untie. He will baptize you with the Holy Spirit and fire.

ENGLISH STANDARD VERSION (ESV)

John answered them all, saying, "I baptize you with water, but he who is mightier than I is coming, the strap of whose sandals I am not worthy to untie. He will baptize you with the Holy Spirit and fire."

GOD'S WORD TRANSLATION (GW)

John replied to all of them, "I baptize you with water. But the one who is more powerful than I is coming. I am not worthy to untie his sandal straps. He will baptize you with the Holy Spirit and fire."

Before the arrival of Jesus, John the Baptist spreads the word of the coming One. He boldly proclaims the truth of Christ the Messiah, the only begotten Son.

*

Mary had just been notified by an Angel from God that she would give birth to the Savior of the world. Upon sharing this incredible news with her cousin Elizabeth, who was also with child, Elizabeth's baby leaps in the womb at the announcement. The cousin of Jesus is excited about the plan of salvation God is about to share with the world.

Even before their respective births, God is preparing the world for the coming Messiah through the message of his cousin John. From the very beginning He will pave the way for the Redeemer who will come into the world to save the people from their sins.

With encouraging words he will share the good news of Jesus to all who will listen, while proclaiming their need for repentance and forgiveness.

John 3:16

KING JAMES VERSION (KJV)

For God so loved the world, that he gave his only begotten Son, that whosoever believeth in him should not perish, but have everlasting life.

NEW INTERNATIONAL VERSION (NIV)

For God so loved the world that he gave his one and only Son, that whoever believes in him shall not perish but have eternal life.

ENGLISH STANDARD VERSION (ESV)

For God so loved the world, that he gave his only Son, that whoever believes in him should not perish but have eternal life.

GOD'S WORD TRANSLATION (GW)

God loved the world this way: He gave his only Son so that everyone who believes in him will not die but will have eternal life.

God's love for the whole world is now revealed through the sending of His Son. A magnificent truth is now proclaimed, He died for us all. He died for each one.

*

We have arrived at the most widely known truth in the entire world, yet its message escapes the multitudes of people on the planet. God is not sending His Son into the world to condemn it, instead He is sending His Son to willingly lay down His life for the sins of all mankind. Through His eternal work of redemption mankind can receive eternal life.

His message is quite simple; no greater love than this that a man would lay down his life for his friends. God declares to mankind that He is willing to lay down the life of His Son so every person in the universe can receive the free gift of salvation whether they be friend or foe.

This miraculous gift from God will separate Jesus Christ from every man who ever walks the earth. Other religions will define what you must do for God to be saved, but Christ will show the world what God is willing to do for you to be saved.

Acts 3:16

KING JAMES VERSION (KJV)

And his name through faith in his name hath made this man strong, whom ye see and know: yea, the faith which is by him hath given him this perfect soundness in the presence of you all.

NEW INTERNATIONAL VERSION (NIV)

By faith in the name of Jesus, this man whom you see and know was made strong. It is Jesus' name and the faith that comes through him that has completely healed him, as you can all see.

ENGLISH STANDARD VERSION (ESV)

And his name—by faith in his name—has made this man strong whom you see and know, and the faith that is through Jesus[a] has given the man this perfect health in the presence of you all.

GOD'S WORD TRANSLATION (GW)

We believe in the one named Jesus. Through his power alone this man, whom you know, was healed, as all of you saw.

Soon, miracles take place, then people are saved and in the name of Jesus, true power is found. The disciples soon discover through faith in Christ; healing, grace, and mercy do abound.

*

Ordinary, sinful men who were once common in the eyes of the world are now performing miracles because they have walked with Jesus, they have gladly received His salvation and now they faithfully follow His word. The power of God's Holy Spirit working through them testifies to the people of the miraculous power of saving grace.

The disciples were eye witnesses to the miraculous works of Jesus. Now they are performing those same miracles amongst the people. The mastery of Jesus working through the lives of these ordinary men is seen throughout the entire region.

The religious, the skeptics and the doubters of the day have no answer for what is happening. All they can do is ridicule or question, but they cannot deny a miracle has taken place. The witnesses are too many and the proof stands before their eyes.

Romans 3:16

KING JAMES VERSION (KJV)
Destruction and misery are in their ways:

NEW INTERNATIONAL VERSION (NIV)
Ruin and misery mark their ways,

ENGLISH STANDARD VERSION (ESV)
In their paths are ruin and misery,

GOD'S WORD TRANSLATION (GW)
There is ruin and suffering wherever they go.

The message is clear to a world caught in sin, that destruction marks the way. However there is a way of escape; repent, receive redemption, and turn your heart over to Christ today.

*

The Apostle Paul appears on the scene to make it abundantly clear, no one searches for God, but God searches for us. He has made known to the world through His creation of His love and presence. He has sent His Son to walk amongst man to declare His plan of salvation for mankind.

Unfortunately many in the world will choose to reject this free gift of salvation offered through Christ. They would rather chase the sin which only offers them suffering and misery.

The world promises much but delivers little, it advertises pleasure but distributes pain and it promotes justice but establishes corruption. The message from Paul is clear. If you choose to follow the world, you choose to be an enemy of God.

1 Corinthians 3:16

KING JAMES VERSION (KJV)
Know ye not that ye are the temple of God, and that the Spirit of God dwelleth in you?

NEW INTERNATIONAL VERSION (NIV)
Don't you know that you yourselves are God's temple and that God's Spirit dwells in your midst?

ENGLISH STANDARD VERSION (ESV)
Do you not know that you are God's temple and that God's Spirit dwells in you?

GOD'S WORD TRANSLATION (GW)
Don't you know that you are God's temple and that God's Spirit lives in you?

After Paul meets the resurrected Savior he proclaims to the believers what the Power of God can do. If you know Christ you are also His temple, His power and Holy Spirit dwells within you.

*

The Apostle Paul proclaims to the church and the world that we no longer need a temple because the Holy Spirit of God lives within us. We are God's temple and through us people can see the work of the risen Savior.

Our bodies belong to Christ and Christ belongs to God, hence our bodies belong to God. What the world says is nothing but nonsense to Him. He commands us to be holy and living sacrifices to Him. We should shun our selfish wants and desires in order to willingly submit to His service.

Christian, are you willing to search your heart and seek what God would have for your life? It is the only life that brings true contentment and happiness. If you choose His way you will not be disappointed.

2 Corinthians 3:16

KING JAMES VERSION (KJV)
Nevertheless when it shall turn to the Lord, the vail shall be taken away.

NEW INTERNATIONAL VERSION (NIV)
But whenever anyone turns to the Lord, the veil is taken away.

ENGLISH STANDARD VERSION (ESV)
But when one turns to the Lord, the veil is removed.

GOD'S WORD TRANSLATION (GW)
But whenever a person turns to the Lord, the veil is taken away.

Paul knew the law of God but his mind had been covered; a veil had separated and kept him away. It wasn't until he realized acceptance of Jesus was the answer; through Christ he found the truth, the life, and the way.

*

Paul shares how he was once a man who was blinded by the traditions of religion. A veil covered his eyes to the truth. After meeting Jesus the Christ the veil was gone. The truth of salvation appeared before his eyes.

The world today is covered by many veils: evolution, science, atheism and false religion. There is a knowledge that brings all understanding, it can be found in a personal relationship with the resurrected Savior.

When Jesus rose from the grave the curtain in the Temple that separated God from man was torn from the top to the bottom. God's act of redemption made a way for anyone to call upon His name to receive a pardon for their sin.

Galatians 3:16

KING JAMES VERSION (KJV)

Now to Abraham and his seed were the promises made. He saith not, And to seeds, as of many; but as of one, and to thy seed, which is Christ.

NEW INTERNATIONAL VERSION (NIV)

The promises were spoken to Abraham and to his seed. Scripture does not say "and to seeds," meaning many people, but "and to your seed," meaning one person, who is Christ.

ENGLISH STANDARD VERSION (ESV)

Now the promises were made to Abraham and to his offspring. It does not say, "And to offsprings," referring to many, but referring to one, "And to your offspring," who is Christ.

GOD'S WORD TRANSLATION (GW)

The promises were spoken to Abraham and to his descendant. Scripture doesn't say, "descendants," referring to many, but "your descendant," referring to one. That descendant is Christ.

The promises made by God to Abraham have most certainly been kept. You too can be blessed and become an heir of God, but first Jesus the Christ you must accept.

*

The Old and New Testament now become one as the forgiveness of sin and the promise of heaven are explained. Salvation is attained through Abraham's descendant, who is known other than Jesus the Christ. God's promise remains true to His people.

Are we so foolish to believe that through our good works we can obtain the salvation of God? It is not through our works but through His righteousness that redemption is attained.

Paul explains how no one receives God's approval by obeying the Law of Moses. It is through the ultimate price paid by Jesus that the promises made to Abraham can be received by all.

Is it time for you to place your faith in the redeeming work of Christ?

Ephesians 3:16

KING JAMES VERSION (KJV)
That he would grant you, according to the riches of his glory, to be strengthened with might by his Spirit in the inner man;

NEW INTERNATIONAL VERSION (NIV)
I pray that out of his glorious riches he may strengthen you with power through his Spirit in your inner being,

ENGLISH STANDARD VERSION (ESV)
That according to the riches of his glory he may grant you to be strengthened with power through his Spirit in your inner being,

GOD'S WORD TRANSLATION (GW)
I'm asking God to give you a gift from the wealth of his glory. I pray that he would give you inner strength and power through his Spirit.

With redemption attained, Paul the Apostle's prayer for you is simple and one short in length. May God give you power through His Holy Spirit and undefeatable inner strength.

*

There is a strength that can only come through the Holy Spirit of God. The love of God is deeper and wider than man can comprehend. It is a love that surpasses all knowledge and understanding.

I pray for you to receive a gift from the eternal wealth of God's abundant glory. He is the only one who can solve your trouble, he is the only one who can ease your pain and he is the only one who can provide to you His grace which passes all understanding.

If you allow Christ to live in you the world will see how deep and wide the love of God is for all. His love goes far beyond anything the knowledge of man can comprehend.

Philippians 3:16

KING JAMES VERSION (KJV)
Nevertheless, whereto we have already attained, let us walk by the same rule, let us mind the same thing.

NEW INTERNATIONAL VERSION (NIV)
Only let us live up to what we have already attained.

ENGLISH STANDARD VERSION (ESV)
Only let us hold true to what we have attained.

GOD'S WORD TRANSLATION (GW)
However, we should be guided by what we have learned so far.

With evil and wickedness all around us, may your walk be narrow and straight. By living up to what you have already learned and attained, the Christ Jesus you can hope to emulate.

*

Paul's message is a clear one. You have a responsibility to live up to the knowledge of what you have attained. Shun the world and keep your eyes on Christ. He is the rock, a very present help in time of need.

Paul was knowledgeable in all the traditions of the Jewish religion and yet he did not see the truth of Jesus until he met the Savior on the road to Damascus.

After meeting the Christ he considered everything else he had learned in his life to be worthless. It was better to throw everything else away in order to attain what Christ had to offer.

Ponder these truths so you can live a life emulating the integrity of the Son of God.

Colossians 3:16

KING JAMES VERSION (KJV)
Let the word of Christ dwell in you richly in all wisdom; teaching and admonishing one another in psalms and hymns and spiritual songs, singing with grace in your hearts to the Lord.

NEW INTERNATIONAL VERSION (NIV)
Let the message of Christ dwell among you richly as you teach and admonish one another with all wisdom through psalms, hymns, and songs from the Spirit, singing to God with gratitude in your hearts.

ENGLISH STANDARD VERSION (ESV)
Let the word of Christ dwell in you richly, teaching and admonishing one another in all wisdom, singing psalms and hymns and spiritual songs, with thankfulness in your hearts to God.

GOD'S WORD TRANSLATION (GW)
Let Christ's word with all its wisdom and richness live in you. Use psalms, hymns, and spiritual songs to teach and instruct yourselves about God's kindness. Sing to God in your hearts.

Our prayer should daily be; may the words of You O God provide wisdom to our hearts, let us be thankful all day long. Help us Lord to teach and admonish one another while praising Your name through glorious song.

*

Our lives should be filled with the richness of God's word. Let our daily walk be centered on the Psalms, hymns, and songs of the Lord. Let us be a thankful people with the peace of God ruling in our hearts.

Our minds should be set upon things above and not encumbered by the troubles of this present world. We have given far too much time to living a life fulfilling our sinful desires.

We are to be humble servants of God imitating the kind, gentle and patient spirit of God's Son, who is Jesus the Christ. Let us forgive others as He has so generously forgiven us.

Thessalonians 3:16

KING JAMES VERSION (KJV)

Now the Lord of peace himself give you peace always by all means. The Lord be with you all.

NEW INTERNATIONAL VERSION (NIV)

Now may the Lord of peace himself give you peace at all times and in every way. The Lord be with all of you.

ENGLISH STANDARD VERSION (ESV)

Now may the Lord of peace himself give you peace at all times in every way. The Lord be with you all.

GOD'S WORD TRANSLATION (GW)

May the Lord of peace give you his peace at all times and in every way. The Lord be with all of you.

My prayer for you is the Lord Himself will grant you peace at all times and in every way. I pray you sense He is always with you and from Him you will never go astray.

*

If you know the Lord then you are a child of the King. Let our lives be the outward appearance of His love for mankind. We need to rapidly spread the truth of God to a world lost in darkness.

Never forget, the Lord is faithful and He will continue to work in your life until the day of His glorious appearing. If we are willing, He will direct our hearts to those who need His life changing message.

Do not be slothful in his service, but whatever you do make sure to do it with all of your might for the glory of God. Labor for His glory and not for your own.

1 Timothy 3:16

KING JAMES VERSION (KJV)

And without controversy great is the mystery of godliness: God was manifest in the flesh, justified in the Spirit, seen of angels, preached unto the Gentiles, believed on in the world, received up into glory.

NEW INTERNATIONAL VERSION (NIV)

Beyond all question, the mystery from which true godliness springs is great: He appeared in the flesh, was vindicated by the Spirit, was seen by angels, was preached among the nations, was believed on in the world, was taken up in glory.

ENGLISH STANDARD VERSION (ESV)

Great indeed, we confess, is the mystery of godliness: He was manifested in the flesh, vindicated by the Spirit, seen by angels, proclaimed among the nations, believed on in the world, taken up in glory.

GOD'S WORD TRANSLATION (GW)

The mystery that gives us our reverence for God is acknowledged to be great: He appeared in his human nature, was approved by the Spirit, was seen by angels, was announced throughout the nations, was believed in the world, and was taken to heaven in glory.

The mystery of God has been clearly revealed to the world through the atonement story. He came in the flesh announced by angels, preached to the nations of the world, rose again from the grave, and was transported to heaven in glory.

*

God's plan of redemption is no secret. His arrival was announced to the world with a hallelujah chorus of angels to the shepherds at Bethlehem. They could not believe what they saw and heard.

Christ then faithfully walked among man performing miracles only God could do. Next the Holy Spirit of God manifested His approval at the day of Christ's baptism.

If the life of Jesus were not testimony enough, His resurrection from the dead should convince you of his Deity. His triumph over death rocked the very foundations of the earth. He displayed to the world there is one way to God and it is through Him.

There is no salvation in any other, Jesus Christ is the only way.

2 Timothy 3:16

KING JAMES VERSION (KJV)
All scripture is given by inspiration of God, and is profitable for doctrine, for reproof, for correction, for instruction in righteousness:

NEW INTERNATIONAL VERSION (NIV)
All Scripture is God-breathed and is useful for teaching, rebuking, correcting, and training in righteousness,

ENGLISH STANDARD VERSION (ESV)
All Scripture is breathed out by God and profitable for teaching, for reproof, for correction, and for training in righteousness,

GOD'S WORD TRANSLATION (GW)
Every Scripture passage is inspired by God. All of them are useful for teaching, pointing out errors, correcting people, and training them for a life that has God's approval.

We can be confident that every passage of Scripture is given by inspiration of God; this is a fact on which you can rely. It is valuable for teaching, correction and reproof; His truths are something that no one can easily deny.

*

You do not walk through this world blindly. You have the inspired words of the Creator at your fingertips. God has preserved His words for instruction in daily living and for power over the evils of this present world.

It began in days of old as Jewish Scribes faithfully transcribed the written word of God letter by letter. No mistake was allowed and precise attention to detail was demanded.

Jesus is the living, breathing word of God in the flesh. When you open the pages of the New Testament, His life changing power mirrors the person we are to become.

Hebrews 3:16

KING JAMES VERSION (KJV)
For some, when they had heard, did provoke: howbeit not all that came out of Egypt by Moses.

NEW INTERNATIONAL VERSION (NIV)
Who were they who heard and rebelled? Were they not all those Moses led out of Egypt?

ENGLISH STANDARD VERSION (ESV)
For who were those who heard and yet rebelled? Was it not all those who left Egypt led by Moses?

GOD'S WORD TRANSLATION (GW)
Who heard God and rebelled? All those whom Moses led out of Egypt rebelled.

Some have chosen to ignore the truth of the word; they have heard and yet they have rebelled. It was the same in the days of Moses with those who left Egypt; their disobedience was unparalleled.

*

There are those who will not believe. They ignore the truth of His coming, they disregard the proof of His resurrection, and they overlook the power of His word. Those who will not hear have rebelled.

Even in the days of Moses there were people who witnessed the saving power of God and yet they chose to rebel. Is God speaking to you? Is His still soft voice encouraging you to choose His free gift of salvation? Do not be stubborn like those who rebelled, but willingly open your life to Him.

Guard your heart. Be careful to never develop a wicked unbelieving spirit that turns away from the Lord of Lords. I encourage you to daily walk in the love of God, making sure to take every opportunity to show His grace to those who are in need of salvation.

James 3:16

KING JAMES VERSION (KJV)

For where envying and strife is, there is confusion and every evil work.

NEW INTERNATIONAL VERSION (NIV)

For where you have envy and selfish ambition, there you find disorder and every evil practice.

ENGLISH STANDARD VERSION (ESV)

For where jealousy and selfish ambition exist, there will be disorder and every vile practice.

GOD'S WORD TRANSLATION (GW)

Wherever there is jealousy and rivalry, there is disorder and every kind of evil.

Even today the world is full of those who are jealous, their selfish ambitions spawn all kinds of evil work. They incite disorder, resentment, and chaos; around each corner their depravity does lurk.

*

James the brother of Jesus now shares an important truth: bitterness, envy, and strife are not attributes of the Prince of Peace. The world is full of those who display selfish ambitions, but those who have the understanding of God will live their lives with humility in service to others.

Does praise and cursing come from your mouth, child of the King? Do you have a temperament of humility or arrogance? A humble spirit is attained through the wisdom of God. Don't boast of what you have done, instead let God boast of what He has done through you.

Look in the mirror today and tell me what you see? Does your life proclaim Him or does it focus solely on thee? Strive to live a life of peace, obedience and mercy, for they are the attributes of God.

1 Peter 3:16

KING JAMES VERSION (KJV)

Having a good conscience; that, whereas they speak evil of you, as of evildoers, they may be ashamed that falsely accuse your good conversation in Christ.

NEW INTERNATIONAL VERSION (NIV)

Keeping a clear conscience, so that those who speak maliciously against your good behavior in Christ may be ashamed of their slander.

ENGLISH STANDARD VERSION (ESV)

Having a good conscience, so that, when you are slandered, those who revile your good behavior in Christ may be put to shame.

GOD'S WORD TRANSLATION (GW)

Keep your conscience clear. Then those who treat the good Christian life you live with contempt will feel ashamed that they have ridiculed you.

As a Christian, please know you will probably be slandered, the world will try to destroy your good name. Respond to them with the love of Christ and your testimony will put them to shame.

*

Now Peter proclaims the humiliation of the world is coming. Those who ridicule the righteousness of the child of God will be ashamed. Do not fear if you suffer for what is right, for in so doing you will be truly blessed by God.

Follower of Christ, revenge is for the Lord. It is not our job to repay evil for the terrible things others have done to us. Our responsibility is to imitate Jesus. Remember His words as He hung on the cross, "Forgive them Father, for they know not what they do."

You must turn away from wickedness and do good. God will see your works and hear your prayers. He will set the record straight. Simply dedicate your life to His service. Let your gentleness, respect and honor for Christ be a shining light in a dark world.

2 Peter 3:16

KING JAMES VERSION (KJV)
As also in all his epistles, speaking in them of these things; in which are some things hard to be understood, which they that are unlearned and unstable wrest, as they do also the other scriptures, unto their own destruction.

NEW INTERNATIONAL VERSION (NIV)
He writes the same way in all his letters, speaking in them of these matters. His letters contain some things that are hard to understand, which ignorant and unstable people distort, as they do the other Scriptures, to their own destruction.

ENGLISH STANDARD VERSION (ESV)
As he does in all his letters when he speaks in them of these matters. There are some things in them that are hard to understand, which the ignorant and unstable twist to their own destruction, as they do the other Scriptures.

GOD'S WORD TRANSLATION (GW)
He talks about this subject in all his letters. Some things in his letters are hard to understand. Ignorant people and people who aren't sure of what they believe distort what Paul says in his letters the same way they distort the rest of the Scriptures. These people will be destroyed.

Some people do not understand these simple truths, so through their ignorance they speak distortion and lies. They do this at their own peril and their very lives they will jeopardize.

*

Do not be carried away with the falsehood of the world. They will try and distort the words of God for their own use. Study to show thyself approved. Be on your guard and grow in the grace and knowledge of the Lord Jesus Christ.

Many will appear and ridicule what you believe. They will ask, where is the prophesied return of Jesus? They will mock and insult your belief in the risen Christ.

Dear Christian, remember this promise. God is patient and He does not want to destroy anyone. He wants everyone to have the opportunity to turn from their wicked ways and receive His free gift of salvation.

Do not be dismayed at their taunting God will fight your battles. He will right all wrongs.

1 John 3:16

KING JAMES VERSION (KJV)

Hereby perceive we the love of God, because he laid down his life for us: and we ought to lay down our lives for the brethren.

NEW INTERNATIONAL VERSION (NIV)

This is how we know what love is: Jesus Christ laid down his life for us. And we ought to lay down our lives for our brothers and sisters.

ENGLISH STANDARD VERSION (ESV)

By this we know love, that he laid down his life for us, and we ought to lay down our lives for the brothers.

GOD'S WORD TRANSLATION (GW)

We understand what love is when we realize that Christ gave his life for us. That means we must give our lives for other believers.

The story concludes as it first began, God showed us the definition of love by laying down His life for us all. Are you, Christian, willing to do the same for your sister or brother; are you willing to answer the Lord's call?

*

The story has come to an end but the message resembles the beginning. Believers are to show the love of God by their deeds and not just by their words. Christ was willing to lay down his life so all might have eternal life, are you willing to do the same? Are you willing to lay down what you want so others might come to meet the Savior?

This is His message from the very beginning. The world may hate you, but God loves you. He demonstrated His love by the sending of His Son. Even though the world was His enemy, God sent Jesus to pay the debt mankind could not pay. Who can truly comprehend the love of God?

You may be the only Bible some people ever read, you may be the only love they ever see and you may be the only voice they ever hear. Christian, what do they see in you?

Revelation 3:16

KING JAMES VERSION (KJV)

So then because thou art lukewarm, and neither cold nor hot, I will spue thee out of my mouth.

NEW INTERNATIONAL VERSION (NIV)

So, because you are lukewarm—neither hot nor cold—I am about to spit you out of my mouth.

ENGLISH STANDARD VERSION (ESV)

So, because you are lukewarm, and neither hot nor cold, I will spit you out of my mouth.

GOD'S WORD TRANSLATION (GW)

But since you are lukewarm and not hot or cold, I'm going to spit you out of my mouth.

As a final show of His grace, through John the Apostle, God provides a warning to the church which has grown apathetic and selfish in an unthinkable way. His message is clear, we are here to faithfully strive with all our might to rescue the perishing; give God your *all*, do not go just halfway!

*

Unfortunately a time has arrived where believers in Christ have become lukewarm. There is no fire or passion to see mankind repent and turn from evil. This is a very dangerous position. Examine your hearts and seek the salvation of mankind. People need the Lord.

It is time for everywhere to humble themselves and pray for the Holy Spirit of God to ignite the fire of truth within the very depths of their heart. Seek God earnestly with a humble spirit of thanksgiving, seek Him daily on your knees and faithfully walk in the light of His word.

If your town, community or neighborhood is ever going to know the story of God it depends on you Christian. Are you willing to show the love of God to those who are perishing? Are you ready to share the story of 3:16?

Epilogue

The game was everything the young man wanted. It had excitement, drama, and in the end, his team left the field victorious. Happy about how the day was going he decided to hang around a little longer and take in the after-game interviews. He wanted to bask in the elation of the moment for just a little while longer.

Near the team bench the sportscasters set up a temporary set for the concluding interviews. This was truly the young man's lucky day. The players would be only a couple of yards from him. He was so close he could hear them speak plainly without the use of the microphones.

As the interviews began, his eyes were drawn to the towel of the team's star running back. It was just an ordinary white piece of terrycloth, but in black marker he could clearly see the number 316 was written upon it. Again with this number, the man was now clearly curious. What could it all mean? He was determined to find out.

When the gridiron great finished the interview he stood up from the chair and began to walk off the field. The young man could not take it any longer, his curiosity had gotten the better of him so he decided to call out to the football star.

"Hey, John, can I ask you a quick question?"

The cleated athlete stopped and kindly said, "Sure, no problem, ask away."

This was his chance to finally find out about the mysterious number, "What does 316 stand for?" The young man knew his grammar was not correct but he did not care, he just wanted an answer.

With a smile on his face, the football great walked over and said, "It means John 3:16. It is a reference to a verse of Scripture in the Bible. When you get a chance you should really check it out, it will change your life." After uttering those words he turned and left the field.

The man knew immediately what he would have to do as soon as he got home. He would have to dig through the closet and find the big black book his grandmother gave him before she passed away. He remembered her telling him it was a Bible and that someday it would play a vital role in his future.

How could she have known that at some point in his life he would be so determined to find out the truth about this text in the Bible? The verse known only to him as 3:16.

About the Author

Dr. Michael T. George grew up in a small town in West Virginia, where the elements of faith, family and hard work were a part of his daily life.

Michael left home at the age of sixteen to pursue a private education in another part of his home state. It is here where Michael's desire to share the powerful story of Christ with others began to take full bloom. Years later he followed the leading of God to attend Andersonville Theological Seminary, where he earned a Masters and Doctorate degree in Pastoral Theology.

More information on Dr. George can be found at MichaelTGeorge.com.

Notes

Notes

Notes